9780837203140
AF575259

THE MIGHTY MIDGETS

written and photographed by Ed Radlauer

BOWMAR PUBLISHING CORP. / GLENDALE, CALIFORNIA 91201

First printing . . . June 1967
Second printing . . . May 1968

The word midget means small, but in midget racing, the action and excitement is big. It takes good driving to handle this Three-Quarter Midget racer, as it slides through the turns on the dirt track.

There are many kinds of midget racing. Here's where it all starts. Quarter Midget classes are for young people, 5 to 15 years of age. Would you say it pays to start young?

Between runs, Quarter Midget cars wait in a place called the pits. Here you can see the hard work it takes to keep in the running. A winning car wins for the racing team as well as the driver.

In Quarter Midget classes the racing team is almost always Dad and a young driver. This gives young folks a chance to learn about cars, engines, and repair work.

Quarter Midget rules require all cars to use the same make of engine. It is a two-cycle engine with a chain drive to the rear axle. For fuel, two-cycle engines use gasoline with oil mixed in for lubrication.

As small as they are, Quarter Midget cars can go up to thirty miles per hour on their short, asphalt track. That is why goggles, jackets, helmets, and strong safety belts are required.

Any car in any midget class must have front and rear bumpers and a roll bar over the driver's head. Nerf bars at the rear wheels keep cars from hooking together. Young or old, these drivers race to win!

These are the Half Midgets, with classes for people aged 12 to 18. Speeds up to forty-five miles per hour are clocked quite often on this dirt track.

Half Midget drivers are sometimes their own mechanics. And what have we here — a curious young lady? No, that's Judy, who is driver and mechanic of her own Half Midget racer.

As in all midget classes, these cars need a push start. Now Dad gets to be a part of the team as Judy in her lucky red car, 38, tries her skill on the track.

In the meantime, other Half-Midget teams are hard at work on the powerful two-cycle engines. Even though smaller, these engines put out more power than those on Quarter Midgets.

Before the final main event race, Judy and other drivers wait in the pits. Friendly arguments about engines, driver skill and winners are what you hear at this time. Before the race, everyone is a winner!

The race is on! All midget racers take a running start in a pack. When the pack crosses the starting line, everyone goes full bore! Keep your eye on Judy in red 38 as she goes full bore.

Oh, come on now, is that any way to treat a young lady? Well, racing is racing and drivers agree that you can't win every race. Better luck next time, Judy!

For those 18 years and older, there is the high speed, high power action of Micro Midget racing. These are dirt track cars which can hit speeds over eighty miles per hour.

In size, the Micro Midgets are not much larger than their little brothers, the Half Midgets. The engines, however, tell a different story. A large, two-cylinder motorcycle engine gives this machine plenty of go.

Another popular power plant for Micro Midgets is this water-cooled, outboard motorboat engine from Germany. This tiny monster can turn 12,000 revolutions per minute to give over 30 horsepower. The tire with the tread is the drive wheel. The other one rolls free.

Midget cars race in classes according to engine size and speed. Drivers make several qualifying laps to be timed. Then they are put in classes according to their best or fastest lap time.

You see interesting body styles among Micro Midget racers. Race crews may build cars as they wish as long as they meet size and safety requirements. This is a roadster body style.

It is not easy to push start some of these powerful Micro Midget engines. Some cars get a push truck for the starting job. Then all the cars gather in a pack for a running start.

Micro Midget drivers must show their skill on the track before they are allowed to race. It takes plenty of practice to handle these small, but very fast cars.

Bigger brothers of the Midget classes are the Three Quarter Midgets, the TQ's. These heavy machines can really move, even on a short dirt track. Two kinds of engines are popular.

A very large motorcycle engine gives this car speed and acceleration. The ridges or fins by the spark plug show that it is air-cooled. The fins carry heat away from the engine.

Some cars get their power from a light, four-cylinder, water-cooled engine. This one is from a small automobile made in our country a few years ago. The carburetor screens keep out dirt.

No, this isn't a tire slasher with a razor. This driver is making many tiny slits between the treads. The slits give the tire extra bite for acceleration and help prevent spin-outs.

TQ Midgets also use a running start in a pack. The raised green flag says, “Go.” A red flag means, “Stop.” The yellow flag says, “Slow down, no passing,” the black, “Get off the track,” the checkered, “You win.”

Well, let's make up our mind which way this race goes! We can see the spun-out driver getting ready to leave his car. First he unsnaps his safety harness. Why the hurry to get out?

Everyone who races Midgets wants to be first to see the checkered flag at the finish line. It not only says, "You win," but it can also say, "You drove a good race."

Everybody who races Midgets wants to have a few of these trophies to put on a shelf at home. Trophies not only say, "You won," they also say, "You drove good races."

But many drive Midgets for more than checkered flags or trophies. The fun of racing is also in being with your friends, other race drivers and crews. Isn't this the real pleasure of any racing?